# Convict Road

by

**Michael Haig**

# Contents

| | page | |
|---|---|---|
| Back in 83 | | 6 |
| Busker | | 7 |
| Jet-ski Rider | | 9 |
| Drive-in | | 11 |
| Shadow | | 14 |
| Broken-hearted | | 17 |
| The Panther | | 18 |
| Derelict | | 19 |
| The Ladies | | 21 |
| Memorials | | 22 |
| Old School | | 24 |
| Shark | | 26 |
| Study in Machines | | 28 |
| Woman Shot Down by Her Husband | | 30 |
| Leave-taking | | 33 |
| Homeless | | 34 |
| Career Paths | | 36 |
| Trafalgar Square | | 37 |
| Bleak Day's Rosellas | | 38 |
| Trespassing | | 39 |
| Discourse | | 40 |
| Holy Man | | 41 |
| Forgotten | | 42 |
| The Wicker Blind | | 44 |
| Willy Willy | | 46 |
| Lines on a Suicide Note | | 47 |
| In the Trenches | | 48 |
| Convict Road | | 50 |
| Winter | | 52 |
| The Artist's Model | | 53 |
| New England Sky | | 54 |
| Sydney Town | | 56 |
| society | | 57 |
| Gold Evening | | 58 |
| Before Mortar and Stone | | 59 |
| On Handing Out Leaflets | | 60 |
| Slessor's Sydney | | 62 |
| The Afternoon Air | | 63 |
| The Prospect | | 65 |
| Patrimony | | 67 |
| Second Heart | | 68 |
| Sydney | | 70 |

| | page | |
|---|---|---|
| The Sort of Eyes You Could Fall Into | page | 71 |
| The Approach of Other Human Beings | | 72 |
| Wishes | | 74 |
| Lost Love | | 75 |
| The Pavilion | | 76 |
| It Was the Fly | | 77 |
| Sydney Season | | 78 |
| Cows | | 79 |
| 1890 | | 80 |
| romance | | 81 |
| In the Morning | | 83 |
| Native Trees | | 84 |
| the inner-city | | 85 |
| windscreen washer | | 86 |
| Tin Can Man | | 88 |
| The New Darkness | | 89 |
| The New Shore | | 91 |
| New Town | | 92 |
| Europe | | 93 |
| God | | 94 |
| The Longboats | | 96 |
| The Clouds | | 97 |
| Quits | | *98* |
| The Lord's Hand | | 99 |
| The Spoils | | 100 |
| The Man | | 101 |
| Voyage | | 102 |
| Becalmed | | 104 |
| Sleep | | 105 |
| Old Furniture | | 106 |
| The Apple-trees | | 108 |
| An Experience | | 110 |
| Border Town | | 112 |
| The Birds | | 114 |
| The Great World | | 115 |
| Sweet Night | | 118 |
| The Pretty Schoolteacher | | 119 |
| Those Days | | 120 |
| The Music | | 121 |
| People | | 122 |
| Homework | | 123 |
| She | | 124 |
| A Letter | | 125 |
| The Season's Song | | 126 |
| One | | 128 |

| | page | |
|---|---|---|
| Tattoo | | 129 |
| Thermometers | | 139 |
| THIS IS JUST A NOTE TO SAY THAT YOU NEEDN'T READ THIS POEM AS IT IS — SO SHORT & SO SWEET ONLY ONE WORD | | 140 |
| Night Sky | | 141 |
| A Summer's Sunday | | 142 |
| Heaven's Waiting-room | | 143 |
| Hurricane | | 144 |
| Exam | | 145 |
| Museum | | 146 |
| Lines: By Philip Larkin's House | | 147 |
| The Cardplayers | | 148 |
| The Garden | | 149 |
| Graduation Day | | 151 |
| Between Four Walls | | 153 |
| Puddle | | 154 |
| Now | | 155 |
| Waves | | 156 |
| Picture Frame | | 157 |
| Letter | | 158 |
| King's Cross | | 159 |
| The Truth | | 160 |
| Memento | | 161 |
| Autumn's Leaves | | 163 |

## Back in 83

and when the world was coming to an end,

back in 83, though waves still rolled round

the wasted worn crust of the world,

and cool collapsing water still seemed tenable

as it struck the barren sand, flowed ashore,

smoothed and glistened, foamed, reversed, and seeped through stones;

what then filled that deadland of blinding heat,

looming like a shade the sunlight lacked,

was the large-limbed woman in suit of black,

gazing from the box-seat of her hair,

standing on one leg, and then upon another,

seeing the horizon as the hours froze,

or the wandering clouds, where they skywards rode:

as though seeing the single fascination

of herself (the close insignificance

of bodies floating on the sand or sea)

— sole surviving remnant of our interest,

final object still standing in the light,

until the sun's last rays expired and flickered out.

# Busker

The busker danced and entertained
the crowd standing round,
and every heart was won,
he swept all clean.

But then came
the audience participation,
the new game
for putting people down,
depressing the heart's elation
— free fodder for no star attraction.
Unwisely, a man whose hair was thinning,
stood in the foremost row.
For all to see
the busker
mockingly supplied his head
with strips of what it lacked.

The man blushed and trembled
with surprise,
and all wandered off laughing
their separate ways.

Later,

a full half-hour later,

strolling the sights

of the gay parade,

you could see the bald man lying,

full-length ways

on a park bench

dozingly in the sun,

a shocked white look of ash

still discountenancing his face,

back-pack sagging at his side

— as though searching

the sun's warm infinitude

the eternal spaces of its separation

or the inner reaches,

the twilit universe and workings,

of his heart and mind

— for the absence

of that hair

upon his head

— for a chance

to begin or perform again

— in spite of all,

to live that lost moment

once again.

## Jet-ski Rider

Hair dolphin-sleeked
until the sun grabs it
to a scruff
in a contained circle he rides
selecting the manoeuvres
from his head
like a filing system
of what might be next in order
— a dolphin-leap nose-diving
to full immersion
re-emerging like a float;
a motored spin, legs hanging loose;
jump of the pale-blue ramp;
smooth arc of the weltering waves.

Thus back and forth he ploughs,
a spectacle apt to disappoint,
a yawn fragrant in your lapel.
Stranded the beached gulls stand
on forlornly tossing pontoons.

Until the show must end,

and there he stands

— a man seeming to do nothing for his pay,

no harvest reaped

from the still wobbling water,

subsiding to stark stillness now,

unspeaking as before.

# Drive-in

Warm on a Saturday night

against the pillows in the car

when summer's freedom drifted endlessly

amongst the largeness of the stars

the huge billboard

spoke into the night.

There was no adventure more massive

to the unsuspecting child

than that jolting jalopy-ride

over drive-in humps,

those earthen shoe-rests

shoehorned to plausible perspectives,

those car-couches

suspended

in entertainment's space,

that astronaut outlook

blast-off ready

at earth's orbit tilt,

clamped to a focus

by the tin-crackling speakers,

mesmerized

in the journey through space.

Balmy summer's breath
swam in one window
and out the next,
lapped
the giant screen,
the sight-board
motioned into space,
and sound washed
the night air
like a still sea
out beyond the groves
of protesting trees
grumbling in pre-history
of withered leaves.
Under the winking dashboard
the car's controls
swaddled more warmth around us
as the actors on the screen
quelled and conquered
the large loneliness
and summer's isolation,
swam in their own story
through the centre of the night.
Until the car's springs bounced us free again
of conditioned entry,
the paddock to be ploughed

back from its days in space.

And now in stranger suburbs,
still more alien worlds,
to lie out in that field again,
on those couches lost at sea,
the voices on the flickering screen
swathing us in sleep
— the comfort of a child
— with parents' voices
on that hill at night,
disconnected to the stars,
would be like attaining
a universe unaltered
— the same stillness of a journey
worth making now
as it was back then.

# Shadow

Shadow,

unoffending friend

in sunlight

or streetlight at night

how many numberless hours

my solitude you've witnessed

the long march

the solitary pain

from youth

to increasing age

the grave's ripe readiness

like full fruit falling

with a wistful regret

and wry foreknowledge

bearing frank congratulation

and complete consent

to every fashion's change.

Underground, then, friend,

cheery soul,

with your spry enjoyment

of every stygian way:

true imprint

following me

none shall know me better

no threat shall darken thee

the hours thus accompanied

unknown hitherto to me

but for you

eternally impressed.

When I rose to meet you

you did not protest or complain

but stood there by

unflinchingly convinced

and perfectly composed

in complete complicity.

At the end of time

we two shall sit together

me with you

and you with me

discussing this

between ourselves

you the everlasting

and me forever growing old

held there eternally in that way

a true reflection

perfectly portrayed

of my infinite possibility

of substantial change

pleasant for the beholder

to behold

when no one's around

when all is loneliness forever

wedded into one

as close as any love

could ever be.

One day I contemplated this

for several hours together

in the slow sojourning sun

and the deep pools of you

seeing how throughout

you perfectly agreed

sympathetically developing

your point of view

from one moment

to the next.

## Broken-hearted

The screams and shouts, the broken hearts
That we too long have rendered,
The tears and taunts, these clutching arts
Mean now our love is ended.

The sleepless thoughts, the hours in nights
Are all we have before us.
To find some rest, to quit these sights
— May God in time restore us!

When love has gone, kind thoughts have flown
Then joy will soon be waning
— And age has come, and sadness grown,
With sorrows swiftly gaining.

So let us then, this wrangling end
That we might be together;
And let us bend our steps again
To ways we went forever.

And this we'll do, old vows renew
— No more be broken-hearted.
We'll keep in view, we're one we two,
So never more be parted.

# The Panther

### After Rainer Maria Rilke

His gaze is filled with such a weariness
of bars, it will hold no more.
One thousand bars and such a dreariness
of hours, he feels, and nothing more.

The soft walk, drunk with stronger
Paces, draws a circle always tighter
Like a dance of power around a centre
In which the will stands stunned, and taut.

Only sometimes folds the soundless
Eyelid higher —. Then the vision makes
Its silent stealthy entrance — when the striding ceases
— And in the heart's core, softly, breaks.

# Derelict

Head pillowed on concrete
I sought my only refuge, sleep.

Lights that never stop burning,
winds that never stop howling.

I dream of a morning,
empty of people,

filled with the sun, filled with the street,
but empty of people.

A lone bird will wander close by
— despised Indian mynah, brown-suited,

black-balaclavaed, yellow claws marching.
Its black beady eyes will look into my eyes,

head cocked and quizzical:
one look, that is all.

Earthbound these birds,
but their eyes know gliding,

windcurrents, high sky riding,
weather-beaten leanness,

the mighty globe's buffets.
But that is all a dream,

stealing through the rain-affected streets
to my head pillowed here,

to my shoulder under
the blanket unpurloined,

never believing the unforgiving concrete,
still waiting for its firmness to flow.

At 6am I move on
through the rivers of twilight,

leaving the dawn discarded,
scrunched on the footpath;

knowing so well the shoes of the city,
my way not with them; falling away,

high or low instead for a dream.

# The Ladies

When he saw the ladies
(the ladies who knew him)
his face lit up with such
a look of beatitude
that our conversation took a whole new turning.

The ladies were wandering
and fussing, looking and ignoring;
and when they took off together
like an orchestra of dedicated birds,
his face retained that look,
such a look of heavenly beatitude
that he turned munificently
as though to bless me,
but found there instead the banal question,
hanging suspended,
there above us,
and his face waned earthly again.

## Memorials

When I was young, there were monuments of stone
— cenotaphs, war memorials, poles of state.
Their public importance was aired out in the sun
— from morning cold, to midday hot, to evening late.

The people should remember, the people should see
the gravity of the message chiselled fair
— the true lines of the nation's history
inscribed on every suburb street and civic square.

But out in the sun the large day burned hot,
and heads were dull, the song of insects was complete.
Under sun so bright, no ray could tie us to the spot
— and the monuments' tale stood silent in the street.

Who could think or even begin to care
for the story of those soldiers set in stone,
who, though fixed fast in iron letters there,
had died in mud or snow so far from home?

For a young country which was well-behaved
a fixed memorial was a duty second-hand.
Doubtless the bitter memory should be waived
as untuneful with the wheatfields in the land.

The whole sky was blue, from one horizon
to the next, yet a single theme ran through:
"We will start our hearts on a new occasion
when times have changed and private thoughts are true."

"For now we will follow this well-worn way
as suiting calculated, careful interests best
— not chosen so that we might seize the day,
but for lost purpose and protection lest."

Our best intentions, then, were put out in the sun.
But the sun gave them credit not at all.
From the blinding heat sheer forgetfulness was won
— and the early onset of a desperate fall.

# Old School

I saw a sparrow fluttering in the yard.
It stood out from the general gliding
by the collapsing fall, the dropping guard,
a frantic fight there was no hiding.

And immediately a brother bird dove
at the bird lying struggling in the grass
— while the host weaved its pattern on above,
far from where the bird was brought to pass.

Did the brother above dive to help him?
or in grief for his brother's plight
soar from on heaven high to meet him?
It was not for that it broke its flight;

for soon a full squadron of birds came down
— repeatedly, too many times, just at the moment when
the lame bird fought to get off the ground.
It was not for pity or for feeling then

that in my human heart and eyes I saw,
nurtured by many books, the beautiful:
but the animal, the rending of a claw,
which even in this sanctuary, this school,

was not foreclosed against, accounted for,
or even half-way towards being understood
— though for that we gained admission at the door,
and though, in the cloister by, so many people stood.

# Shark

Ten feet from the shore when the shark came
as I bobbed up from the sea's floor

scraping for star-fish, sea-shells.
Moving terror the big fish came

— creature without a man's means of handling
— freak happening, black rumour's realization.

The fluid form possessed my brain
for the taut moments' rapt attention.

No way to bargain with a beast
— the one-way channel of the jaws.

The animal cunning of my human form
— the faculties are sure in face of danger.

To the aroused senses the absolute comprehension
of each morsel of information.

My life my imagination was a marooned island
peaceful in the untrammelled sun

— but circled by the sundering seas,
sorry for my vast adventure.

And so I sojourned there in the swelling water
like a cork, like a bobbing buoy in water,

thus remote form the aspect of fodder,
like a sea-snail, like any sea creature

— camouflage of my human cunning.
The marooned island was my prayer to God

— to live all one's life thus,
in the stillness of the savage waters

— the gaiety of the peopled shore
hoving off with the stunned force of an idea.

So the shark circled with an absolute command of its own
— as compliant to contemplate

as the brute seas from a distance on their own.
Until it was no more.

## Study in Machines

The men with their machines work on the construction site.
The shovel gouges soil.
It is a cautious hand, careful to perform
an awkward action, at the level of constant proficiency.
Machines go wrong but unlike the beast of burden
— rounding wild nature upon its master
— its wrongness consists in this
— currents of control will unfurl, uncoil,
unleash sparked protestations of bile
— its absolute unarguable intention, fastidiously foreplanned,
will tear body and blood.
The machines realize bold proposals
but the reality is petrified tender care.
In due order scrupulously observed
the trucks back onto the shovels
proffering passively
their capacious saddle backs.
The shovels load up the dirt, smoothing,
combing, carefully adjusting the load
orchestrating a knobbed quiver of levers and pedals
like a campanologist dashing among his bevy of bells;
thus the slave spills never a drop
of the master's stoup of liquor.
In this manner hours pass.

Like tamped-in tobacco

the loads are carted away

to distant destinations.

The driver slopes off to smoke,

his machine still chugging,

accepting the dirt.

He rests his mind, eyes behind shades

among the toughness of dirt;

the peripheral heaviness of massy

truck doors, resistant gear levers,

cogs and controls,

as the coward back from the war

— the smoked confusion, the uncertainty and chaos

— can recall forever onwards how he was a hero.



Note: Machines can only effect a transformation of matter; not like animals which are able to be bridled (and cannot be switched off), and give birth, and are part of the food-chain. Animals possess animus (will and avoidance—a relation of life and death); whereas machines transform inanimate matter with an animus (fuel) which is strictly controlled. Breakdown of machine can indicate machine's dependence on animus. So duration of machine's operation, except for breakdown, can lack the quality of will/avoidance and response which animus has.

## Woman Shot Down by Her Husband

He got up early, the plan was in his head.
Liberty's last dawn shone yellow and red.
In the ordinary course he put on coat and tie
— not dressing for death, not he to die,
but for the morning's old simplicity,
unravelling night's complexity.

Private was the business he had to settle.
The day would disclose and prove his mettle
— equal to the deed. O down to death!
Though the bullets rose from the hand to wrest
life from the woman whose womb had borne
two sons, one daughter — children time-wise torn

to live upon this earth — to follow footsteps
that went before not after — quicksteps
over sandy shallows, in the brightly blue,
not this mud-soaked horror from the gun he drew.
Their hearts fell with her when she fell
— their happy home, their hearth, their citadel.

Gun's nozzle invested with authority.
History's halls quiet in time's austerity.

The gun speaks out dog-like, it is true,
but flesh is complex that the holes run through.
The frame spills blood, much more within is knit
than spinning, whistling shells ever could hit.

Those projectiles single-mindedly flung
from the holding hand, those heroes most unsung
sent forth from the weapon's obstinate o,
the body's shape, soul's story, could not know,
for flesh is bloody, while the mind is not
(yet the mind thinks the bullets that the hand has shot).

And who had won? Was more fortunate she,
who went down by the bullets slain, than he,
remaining on this earth, to feel the sun's reproach,
high in the sky, above the night's approach?
The bullets hugged her as she caught them,
her own blood undid her as she fought them.

No time to appeal, she was on her knees,
entirely woman, begging the sweet breeze,
stunned by the bullets' searching intimacy,
sharp criticism, cast-off contumacy,
breathless with too much force, hate's after-storm
— never more to be cold, never more to be warm.

The event is held forever as it was,
in time's album, unaccompanied by because.
He pocketed his weapon, and he smiled,
all the hard heart within him beating wild.
The stone years rose up before him as he turned,
and all the endless agonies he had not learned.

## Leave-taking

With packed bags, clasped bags
to get the show on the road,
here, in this little town, time drags
and she is ready to go.

But as she stepped outside,
set her first foot on the lawn,
a little bird descried
a song inside the dawn.

No matter which road you take,
the end of each is death;
no matter the friends you forsake
or make, till your last drawn breath

in a fast world you cannot
escape the mockery of return;
fate which the powers allot
the ribbon roads cannot unlearn.

# Homeless

Body broken by concrete, the homeless man came.
His house was in his bag, to which he clung.
Portable plastic convincing colours but he was lame.
Bark blasted by the sun, on the scrapheap flung.

He crept, he crawled, he was at an end.

Nothing that the doctors could do with a frame
that boasted flesh cured like meat on a hook.
No manipulation massive enough to undo the shame
that the world had done. One had to look

at the man of the burnt desert in the streets,
at the twisted leather of an old shoe gone to boot.
The streets are empty where the shopline greets
the sky (shops below jealously guarding their fruit).

Uncertain I regarded him where he stumbled
and where he stepped how his humanity almost
rolled down to his knees, the private part of him humbled
— how with difficulty he sat with his own trouble engrossed.

He moved aside his still abundant hair.
A wound on his eye blossomed folds of skin

and harsh nature's unreadiness to repair

in a body so broken one wondered what coursed within.

Still I looked, and he fetched back a look
sharply to warn me off the place he had.
Immediately I returned to read my book
but the look struck my mind as sad

— lighted rooms, thoughts which fed it said
doors which closed — ingress egress
but to this park in a desert his life had led
to displayed loneliness, disregarded distress.

And so we sat in the sun and I felt my bones
where they sat, and life went on over it.
His life was smashed like shattered stones
on a dry river's bed. His life was lit

with unkind streetlight. His bed had fallen
on hard times and manufactured stone
— but sunlight soothes the appalling...

## Career Paths

People in cars with money

don't care about the streets

dark in between the walls.

Driving in on a Saturday night

after a party with friends,

they drive into the danger zone,

huddled together, in their hearts afraid,

but with money to buy off danger.

But in the dark, disregarded streets

danger breeds and stalks

creeping just out of the light.

They flirt with it, court it,

over drinks with friends.

Without it their lives are void

— safe houses, safe jobs

by computer terminal, by in-tray.

They need the danger,

but will not meet it on its own terms

—taste but not devour,

tantalize but not consume.

## Trafalgar Square

In Trafalgar Square the pigeons flew.
One of them stood out:
a huddle of tattered feathers, unable to fly
— a limping waddle, balding head
hunched into its shoulders.
Miserable wretch,
only good for a peck on its balding bonce.

That such a wretch should live!
Beneath Nelson's Column!
Sustained only by the plenty of the place.
The brother birds let him know it
— savaging his bald patch,
enraged by his meanness
— a slight to our plumage
— our sleekness, our smooth gliding,
our gracious flight, our glorious show.

# Bleak Day's Rosellas

Rosella for the green leaves of the tree.
Rosellas in the midst of trees
as though the space of the grey sky
and the dull leaves washed with rain
were the measure of their colour
— yellow brought from the sun,
green from the bottom of the sea.

And given wings.

The surprised trees, clear
in gleaming droplets
were placed for the movement
of colour
akin to spirit.

# Trespassing

To trespass in the small hours
of the afternoon
down mossed-over lanes
and avenues no longer mown.

To wander in the lost days of June
where the trees are set out in rows
and cars are parked by the road.

In front of a lost house,
three dancing butterflies
weaving the scent of flowers.

## Discourse

We talked in the empty room

by the windows

and the conversation turned

to a topic guided by the hidden will.

As I went down this way

sex stalked into the room

from beyond the window pane,

and I knew there must be a killing,

claws must make a showing.

This was suggested by the news we heard.


So where now should I take my bleeding?

# Holy Man

One day my path crossed
that of a holy man of the East.
My way was not lost,
but my anger rose like yeast,
in fierce frenzy of the West,
to see his passing footsteps pressed.

In my own land he took
a way different from my own.
Senseless even to look
— a sullen stone thrown
across the park.
The clothes he wore were dark.

# Forgotten

When we posed the question

requiring an answer yes or no

remarkably then we felt the course of time

underneath the light-shade

in the dining-room late at night.

We were amongst the stars

drifting between planets

the curls of hair beside your cheeks

flecked with light

the wonder of creation

so distant it was forgotten

convinced that it never was

yet promised here again

the light of the electric bulb

not divorced from the light

at the centre of the world.

In a sense I cared for you

though me you affected to despise

and the despite for me you created in others

was painful and real.

I will not forget

though surely you have done so

and though in spite of my words

you did not wish me well,

I will not forget

the curls beside your cheeks

the flecks of electric light

within the curls and on your cheeks

and the journey in time

between the planets amongst the stars.

## The Wicker Blind

when in all the world you lacked a friend
when no one gave you life to mix or mend

a stream of thoughts ran through your head
— one last connection, one last coherent thread

to unravel for the meaning following on
like a line of horses pounding, pounding on

no other way than this the days were spent
— deep-delving the catacomb of argument

unloading the heavy logic of ideas
imaging the steady swaying of the trees

so it was when none you called a friend
when all good time and company were at an end

when the wide world was only good for sitting in
when each new neighbour was your next-of-kin

only in the wind and sunlight of the street
like the constant sway of a field of wheat

the wicker blind moved back and forth
— a salutation of the wind in leaving earth

but no soul would ever see to know
the play of wind and light, of light and shadow

— the constant agitation of the breeze
(the freedom in the thought of trees)

this was the only pleasure that remained
while the waving of the wicker was sustained

this was the only society that survived
— the ending undulation while the wind arrived.

# Willy Willy

A still day though the cicadas rang

when the willy willy rose,

A chill in the heat, the brown man

in a swirling coat

in his peregrination past this place,

a whirlwind, spoken in a tongue

by the traveller, the stranger,

hill climber, hill stalker

over sticks and stones,

the ancient hillside.

It blew the curtains inwards,

held us presently in thrall,

a message from God,

given breathtakingly

in a twist of wind.

# Lines on a Suicide Note

Was there nothing left to live for, the old man
— no hidden agenda, yet to be revealed plan,
that he left this place with only a note
no human being ever conceived or wrote,
explaining how the heartache such news conveyed
would never be discussed, resolved, allayed?

For he was gone for good, he would be dead
by the time the note was perused or read.
Did no hand reach in from beyond the grave
attempting to amend the lines it gave
repenting quickly that he had been so cruel
to send ahead he was beyond recall?

Did no living claim lay fast hold on him,
to arrest his entry to beyond earth's rim?
No sheer adherence to the flesh he wore
(life's only access to certain death's door)
assailing the resolution he assumed
that even simple daylight could be doomed?

# In the Trenches

In the trenches I saw my brother
bathed in blood
or shivering in mud
in a hole in the wall;
eating from a rusted tin.

I remembered a time
from the days of peace
when my brother was not my brother
but a lord
doing himself proud
playing foolish games
distant
in his own world
making his own way
a companion to men
who shared only his self-absorption.

This memory became
a kind of bitter reminder
of what we had to find
in the trenches
— of what we were too self-absorbed and foolish

to find in the good times

during fair weather

and fair prospects.


How poor is the state of man

that he must needs

crawl below ground,

surround fair bodies

with fear,

torment the vision and the mind

with torn limbs

and mangled flesh

and damaged lives.

Create a situation

of pain and desolation,

only to remind himself

that men eat, sleep, die,

that they live on bread,

not pomp and circumstance

or nationhood,

and that by forgetting the bread,

they forget what there is

in addition to bread.

# Convict Road

On the convict road
the convicts' ghosts
are roaming. Cluster,
flock thick and fast
to joints of stone and wood.
Their shackled fists are hammering.

Only the convicts stayed true, kept the siege,
the sad, spare souls of the convicts standing,
wryly smiling, milling round their earthworks still,
waiting for restitution, their bloody mouths, food-filled,
demanding satisfaction, battening their wills
on the works built with their own hands,
still hammering their iron voices on the anvil stone.

The souls of the convicts lounge out in the sun,
crowd thick in the sun, raising a hubbub,
a muttering vexation. Press close
to familiar ways — known hankerings,
pet hatreds, kindred desolations;
together on the cool green alleys of the way,
where the gums haze in eucalypt,
lean in blurred and solipsistic song.

Instinct with this earth,
the convict road is winding,
its curves and corners true.
Forging its question
on the landscape still.

# Winter

So winter comes
one day in the morning:
and he is an old curmudgeon
trailing his beard in the trees.

From the garden
we must fetch the white chairs
and the table; then tie to the banks
our slow summer craft;

for now is the time
of an old man's wishes,
now is the time
for his tantrums and storms;

and we will have none of him!
But the earth, it seems, loves
an old man's spite
and the river frowns indulgently.

## The Artist's Model

was a seventy-five years old man.

I wondered what was going through his mind.
He must have seen two world wars.

What were we through his eyes?
How did he, from position nudity, see us,
dressed in the superiority of clothes?

# New England Sky

It was sunny in the morning,
the clouds were way up high
— inside the library looking
at a clear New England sky.

The day had turned out perfect,
the pipes of zephyr softly played;
the balmy weather at a surfeit,
the boughs of branches sweetly swayed.

Still my studies were my interest
as towards them then I turned
— to glean the steady answers,
what the foremost minds had learned.

Through the pattern of the pages
a living story I could trace
— of the decline and fall of ages,
the next ascent of every race.

So my thoughts began to brighten
as the story could unfold,
and knowledge was enlightened
while the tale was truly told.

But, then, in spite of seeming glory

the heart yet tends to weep

— considering the human story,

its occasional sense of leap.

For life-time's truly bitter,

its ending's brutish brief

— man's condition's lost and little,

his career goes down with grief.

So to leave the books there lying

on the tables where they came

seemed what the words were saying

in several senses all the same

— when beyond the breeze was blowing,

the sultry season sailing high,

with every answer flowing

from a blue New England sky.

# Sydney Town

We sight-saw the suburbs
cloaked in dust and heat,
ascended and descended
the slow-rolling hinterland of hills
— the carapace that crawled inland
and sulked in silence.

But what remains
of Sydney that summer
once the vacation weeks had passed
is the image
of the old man knocked down
out walking his dog
— a line of cherry blood
burgeoning on his brow,
running a red river down
— like the first part of that summer
flowing from its last...
a final message
from the heart that grieved
of Sydney town.

## society

in my time in time immemorial
there proved to be nothing worth remembering:

descend to all forgetting
was the name of the game.

For people there would be no recalling
the writing of their names,

no path was worthy
the treading of one's feet,

nor meal was salted
with society of a friend:

for we had dedicated our lives
to matters subterranean

— deep-sea diving
for a bone

# Gold Evening

The evening was gold on the Hammersmith Bridge
the day I took a stroll
and found the way
through the subway beneath the road
— to the banks of the river
— a private lock, a sculling club
and boats lolling upon mud
— stones and river-dirt
sanctified by time
on the level only
of human memory and emotion
— a vision splendid in the gold
of the evening in the fretwork
of the Hammersmith Bridge.
And yet I did not speak
to the people there,
but passed on without a word,
since they sat round like the guardians,
the ones who remembered,
and I was the intruder,
having solved a conundrum
made mysterious and deadly
in the sand of a different shore.

## Before Mortar and Stone

Lonely room, a prison self-built
— legs lying idle on the quilt,
noises of neighbours in the hall,
propped with my book against the wall.

    Yet the wind is gentle, uncertain,
stirring the lace curtain,
with the neglected spirit of God.
Kind face at the window,
ushering up,
invisible,
an untasted cup,

something before mortar and stone.

## On Handing Out Leaflets

What I had to offer was nothing much
— leaflets for discounts on books at the store,
yet the responses of people was such
as to give pause to consider it more.

Some took it with a smile or at a run,
some looked distressed, confused, or merely blank,
some as though I held at their guts a gun,
some found it not too difficult to thank.

When one did not take, the others followed suit,
cringing by the wall, as though under fire.
When one was unsure, the others were mute,
and many the leaflets dropped in the mire.

Through the face they made up for the street
flashed at times the hidden emotion they felt.
My job was only to give them the sheet,
but something else was beginning to melt

— denial, or need, or a combination
of these, in the story their faces told.
Perhaps they well knew their destination;
perhaps they had no need to have or to hold.

But what I wished was to give them a key
— a key that should infallibly unloose
their cares and troubles, the pain that we feel:
for the yoke is light, but heavy the noose.

## Slessor's Sydney

Stiff leather, stark leather, fashion for feet;
silk ties, smart ties, cufflinks and winter wool;
gelatine, brillantine, a barber's stool;
sun-parched in the smog-dust of Flinder's Street.

Besides the steady encroachment of dereliction,
gentleman's fashions and ladies' gowns
— apparel for the people about town
— good taste, fine humour, predilection.

Public servant in governmental stone;
sandstone self-importance in the bright sun;
exactly where the creeks of Crown land run;
the dead wood, the vacant miles, the bleached bone.

Shirts of pure cotton, silk and fine satin;
migrant tailor with a small clientele;
seams on a shoulder, and fashioned quite well;
hems on a shoe-front, stitched on a pattern.

Slessor's Sydney still under the blue sky;
the windows need cleaning, the doors open wide;
not featured in photos, press or a guide;
lost in its day-dreams, deep down is street shy.

## The Afternoon Air

Beautiful face of the woman on the train
caught my gaze for a moment,

registering the look that registered
beauty, but giving it no great account.

And so she sat in front of me:
beautiful, wild hair,

cut short, she'd tamed herself,
self-tamed.

Then she sat by the window
while the train scythed its metal arc.

Sun through the window,
sun in the hair blown by the breeze

of the afternoon air,
to reveal the made-up face

— colour on the cheekbones
and around the creaturely eyes.

Self-tamed: the wave in the hair,

at a certain length, in a certain style

— but the breeze of the breath of sun
through the window

— fields where children played;
hard edges, sudden corners;

the turned page, bent covers;
stairs climbed and decisions made.

But the breath of sun in the hair
of the woman, self-tamed this time.

## The Prospect

"Working the seam of words for fifty years,
and how many words live, aspire,
surface to the page's living blankness,
sifted from the mire?"

So said the old prospector,
his stooped back turned to us,
knee-deep in water, pan in his hands,
unwilling to let a single grain pass

uninspected,
unturned-over,
unworried-at,
unaccounted-for.

Since he waded in this stream
all those many years ago,
he's had reason to regret,
misgivings to bestow

upon the youthful sparkle in his eye,
glinting like the gold it saw
on the river's shallow bottom
those o so many years before.

"One story, one poem, a handful
of words is all I've got to show,"
said the old prospector to us then.
"But stay on I must, I cannot go

— only the flame of sudden wealth
can feed the emptiness within.
There's no going back
to where you were, once you begin.

Some may learn from this richness
that I glean you; see what I see;
but let the river's wisdom drown me
when all is done — and so let be."

# Patrimony

Alien in my own household,
alien in my own city
— streets without gold,
eye without pity.

No face acknowledges,
no kith is kith, or kin kin.
Sole citizen of my own country,
guarding the last citadel within

— confederate with my own soul only,
the last post of timelessness is near
— the end of all connection,
functioning flesh, pumping fear.

## Second Heart

When, in neither language that they spoke,
she brought herself, dressed demurely, to the door
(remembering words he had said before),
it was the second heart that broke
— heart of melancholy,
heart of dream;

while the first heart flared up in rage
to feel such flat denial of the time,
such bare-faced denial of the crime
— <u>it is war, it is war we wage</u>!

It was too late, it was far too late
for denying the lately consummated scene
with memory of what they once had been.
That was pure rejection of their fate.

<u>We must find love: love will make us one</u>,
she'd said; and he'd believed with second heart.
But it was first heart then to take the devil's part,
divining no escape beneath this sun.

<u>What is love, when love must reach an end</u>?
he said, and turning, found the door.

And what are these trysts and truces for,
when need is none for lover or for friend?

The wide world is where we all belong.
To wander or take wing is all I care,
as freely as the breeze or air,
closing the door, he said, and so was gone.

Decision was, tomorrow he would leave:
but her appearing seemed done to win him back,
foreseeing the pang of loves that lack
(broken dreams, sweet broken dreams we weave!)

Beyond the room lay the alien town.
Arrival, departure, were easily done.
His leaving now would be speedily won.
The elevator, directly, would take him down.

So departed, she saw him from the window-ledge,
scanning both ways at the kerbside edge
— a tiny, walking figure ten floors below
— no one, whom, not knowing, she would ever know;
and remembered to herself such words he'd spoken
yet truly, how her lonely heart was broken
— heart of melancholy,
heart of dream.

# Sydney

Sydney from Melbourne was a harsh arrival.
For a Melbourne boy it was God's own reason
that comrades would respect your pain.
But Sydney people had grown strange in houses,
despising all one's love.
How could it be that they had found a way
of not caring that you went away.
"Let's play football while the sun is high
 — just one game before lunchtime calls."
"No, I won't" — and then yet more grievous sin:
"Ring Richard, why don't you call him up
 — I'm tired, you go away and play with him."
And then shut the door and turn within
and face all friendship out with sleep and silence
and say nothing more except the wordless door
 — a closure without any rhyme or reason
or further sequel.
So going home was all that you could do:
to reconcile yourself to Sydney and its seasons.

## The Sort of Eyes You Could Fall Into

on the bus on its way down george street,
it was said: the sort of eyes you could fall into
— "dark and..."; and her words were sweet,
beyond the hurly-burly humdrum we were driving through,

the toiling busy streets we were falling through
— she and I; though her words were not mine
and the eyes were not mine, which she had in view
— streets beyond view, world beyond time.

in the darkness of those eyes, a dream in flesh,
twilight of sleep where all is resolved;
where all destinies and absolutions mesh

— this (and so much more) seemed from her voice evolved.

## The Approach of Other Human Beings

never brings the long-sought-for assurance
of fellowship, understanding, friends indeed;
but more often brings a life's endurance
of exactly the opposite of your need.

At first, then, there's humiliation, blame,
cruelty apparent in each man you meet,
a manifest intent to wound and maim,
and enemies that lurk down every street.

But when we've searched for a new relation,
find not better ways to better means, but
a similar pattern still pervading,
the familiar dogs flying at your throat.

Yet when we've sought help and due attention,
strike not the waters that life is craving,
but fresh founts of hate's hot derision,
the certain shores infernal lakes are laving.

And though we've hoped for some small change of fate,
discover there's none that shall e'er agree:
for being different now's to start too late:
you'll never get remorse, there'll always be

the same adherence to a pack of lies,
no matter what one does, how hard one tries;
leaving nothing but wanting to devise
any desperate scheme to minimize

the approach of other human beings.

## Wishes

If only it was always winter,
no time passing swiftly below
the pond at the end of the road
(children who dream ingenious games,
slipping and sliding and finding snow).

If only there were just one colour,
no spring imprisoned underground,
then, my love, I should be happy,
not wanting, not needing you, only listening
for your footsteps, leaving without a sound.

## Lost Love

Though we have lost love, love won't let us go,
But stays between us, pandering to our pain.
Though memory proves the hurt, the heart says no:
Only one will do: we must meet again.
Though the rope has slackened with the years,
The slackening brings a tightening of the will
To end this; yet the mind is weak with fears,
For time breeds hope while time has stripped our skill.

If love is what I find of me in you,
Why can't I tear it out and set it free?
Or is it just reflection which we view:
We turn away and lose the eyes that see?

Yes, my own love, the force of love is strong:
We love—I do not think that we are wrong.

## The Pavilion

Matted weeds and tangled nettles
behind a rusted gate, in a shed of brick
by a river running softly, smoothly,
are all we find, once the meaning settles.

The key was lost many years ago:
in the dead gardener's pocket, in a chest of drawers,
in a house we shall not inhabit
down a roadway in the valley there below.

There was a vision in the dusk
of fine-clipped lawn and people
— a hand trailing from a boat upon the river.
The germ of the idea became its husk.

Pavilion daubed with yellow letters,
built for a purpose
abandoned by the river,
the ruthless runners and the go-getters.

Wild weeds grown long and tall
obscure the purpose once clear and bright.
The prison of the nettle, the crumpled leaves,
rampant in the enclosure of the wall.

## It Was the Fly

that spoilt the poem.
It came buzzing, uninvited,
round my cone of pensive light,
taking my thoughts hither and thither,
unravelling through the room:

until I stood
to open the door
and let it out,
free forever of every conceivable
distraction.

## Sydney Season

Bright blossom and fierce fragrance
— Azalea, Camelia, Camphor Laurel.
Tangle of green, fierceness to entrance.
Neither spring nor autumn
but the true time of summer
which winter gaoled but weakly.

# Cows

Cows carousing round a trough
are happy enough.

Cows playing hornless push and shove
are cows in love.

Cows mirroring cows
are seeing cows.

Cows stumbling through the pack,
jump on each other's back.

Cows standing in a huddle
want to make a puddle.

Cows in the furthest paddock
expect the traffic.

Cow and cows and cows and cows
— no one disallows.

Cows in heaven: cows in trouble:
hope I'm only seeing double.

# 1890

I remember the face of my brother who died,
his face on the pillow blank and pale.
Upon the cushion when my tears have dried,
I hold this flickering image of him now
like a leaf which stirs upon the bough
— in a winter wind, in an autumn gale.

When the age of photographs came to pass
— I could not be sure how they should be used
those faces trapped forever under glass.
So far as I could see it was another
— brother, sister, father, mother
— dead in a sickness they could not refuse.

To remember then seems better than to see;
for eyes are angry, while the heart forgives.
Better with dying to forget, be free.
Now the photograph seems all I have, and,
there it is — there it lies upon my hand
— dead, as the forgetting in my heart still lives.

## romance

our love was all a dream
we thought we'd never die,
surmounting every challenge,
younger the next time round,
more glamorous.
in the newest scene
we'd play the leading part.
like super-heroes,
roles that would never end.

and now we persevere,
searching through streets
for some better action,
together at heart,
still believing
our luck will never end.
one day we'll fix those bickerings.

or is it like those sci-fi movies
or action-packed high-speed adventure
— where the hero runs low
of ammunition,
rifle, or cross-bow all but spent,
still loading the barrels
the last cartridges,

scraping the bottom

of the barrel or the bag,

while the innumerable enemy,

outmatching the power of his draw,

begins to crowd

the valley or the rise,

and the hero sees

with pained and urgent eyes,

not clear on the desperate horizon,

if he will escape,

seize a fresh supply,

or this time lose it all?

## In the Morning

the light came,

and the birds,

the people singing

in a kind of air-current

such as birds swirl in.

The light came

to lift the darkness

lying on me, tombstone-heavy,

in the morning

at the end of night

# Native Trees

Native trees do not witness weather
but stand there haggard, livid in the sun
— haphazard groves clumped together,
tree indistinct from tree, and each from everyone.

Sooner become a settler of the moon
than grow down to these sticks and stumps.
Civilization came to these shores too soon
to make these savage jumps.

## the inner-city

as close as we came was looking through
the windows of other people's houses
— a pure purview swiftly turning blue
of people without their skirts or trousers

we had not grown up to understand
the need all had for one another
— we never recognized the first demand
to accompany a sister or a brother

streets were complications
unthinkable to return
to the simple purity of a room
limitless in all directions

dulled ambition turned awry
in a late-night café over coffee
— coffee a convenient way of
never admitting you were sorry

## windscreen washer

not at school, not clear where she may be
the little girl washes car windscreens for a living
as the traffic waits, as the traffic flows, a wash for fee
no greater ambition, no more that she should be giving

than this moving between cars, innocently gambolling,
smoking a cigarette, bare legs and curves
all that she has to give, sexability outstanding,
in a moment of the day, heat of the hour, perhaps the eye swerves

as the car swerves, plant that's still growing,
distracted, abstracted, view of local happening
in the prospect now, seed of the new millennium sowing
high school graduate, one of the new, latter-day

sixteenth century poor, yet to be discerned,
perhaps never to be discerned by the uncaring
city men in suits going down fast to be learned
by such as she was, so pleasantly faring

to the end of the line, affecting to know
their fat security might protect them still
the drift of their cowardice and greed still might flow
to the safe port, to sweet dreams under the hill.

They were thinking it wouldn't hit them
— the poverty straps, the junkyard out the back.
They'd go down and fail to last the distance
— before the ghetto in-gathers, before the poverty shack

# Tin Can Man

Take an empty man,
fill him full of denial,
rattle him with blows,
he is a tin can now,
the metal sides you hammered
with demented disregard
eyes glowing turned back
penetrating the tin can skin
the denial oscillating there
coming a little closer
rolling the shoulder over
lifting the sack full the rattling
rattling on inside.

## The New Darkness

The new darkness was a still, sunlit day
of those of us who survived
only footsteps fell on the new earth
gazing with curiosity about us
in the riversand
we heard the footsteps and saw each other
in the new land where there was no food
the empty newness was hunger
but inside us there was none
it was all around us so the body had rest.
At least we lived to see it
but the passing of what was
was travail was the world's judgment upon us
piercing us with shafts of bitterness
battered with reproach.
At least we lived through it
only wishing to live through it
to be shut of it,
let the old worm die.
We are less than we once were,
the hair, the faces, the clothes, unchanged,
but we are less
and where now we live in a place
of bare necessity sparing the mind its thought

here and there still inhabit
people of the old world
to remind of what now we must avoid
and still we find the rasping cry
of the palled power of what was
dwindling spectacularly to a tinker's cuss

Each running towards the light,
mouths open, the running was ecstasy,
famished frenzy groping in sand.
We dug right through
— through the old world and into the new
and we were there all unchanged,
in the familiar light, with gulls about us
crying emptiness
crying sand beneath our feet;
walking slowly after the frenzy
into the arms before us open wide.

## The New Shore

floating up to the new shore,

the newness of the gulls' whiteness

the inverse of the pool

either heavy with too much thought

or light with the gulls' spareness

ever on the underside

actual or unreal, biding the time

of the lightness of blown paper

# New Town

The new town is an old town,
gathered scraps of the old world
assembled a fire
things uncared for look old when new
makeshift the design, ramshackle the execution
what dwells within harbours its imperfection
postpones the time of execution
resentment grudges, petty resentment
when together trammelled
a paling fire odious to those above them
but bear the signs of their own becoming,
the smouldering ring of an ineffectual fire
are the flames of what may come.

## Europe

the broken wings of Europe

where was the emblem we would find

on the roads and country miles

abruptly tarmaced over

— brown broken walls abandoned by the city

and the people, scaffolded neglectfully,

littered equitably

through the muddled streets, by alien shores,

the gateway free and unperturbed,

in the broken interior we found

broken like the broken light of freedom

the broken wings of Europe

# God

At the ultimate age of thirty three
the realization dawned moot sure to me,
your sins are many
better it were
you had not any.

Regretfully
I thought on those fortunate few
who when fresh-faced young directly knew
better it were
to be most clean
never to be seen
transgressing — who had the requisite fear,
knowing back then to keep right clear.

but then the angel of the Lord said to me
there is no mortal that has been
in whom no blot though slight were seen
— though your sins are many
and indeed it is better
that there were not any
God forgives though man does not
so keep on straight and true like Lot.
Sin you may again
and we shall take counsel then

but do not despair

your life repair

and do not give ear

to those that cannot hear

nor heed my first-thought call

— my desire is to save you all.

Most surely blessed they be

and, though my anger you have earnt, you shall see

the greatness of my might and mercy free.

## The Longboats

When the longboats came ashore
there were different birds abroad
singing the songs to a new heaven

## The Clouds

Nimbus, cumulonimbus, cirrus,
clouds in their glory when I was a boy

Cirrocumulus, cumulus fractus,
towers in their kingdom, none could destroy

Not the clouds in their whiteness
not the sun in its brightness
when I was a boy
but the names climbing multiform
the clouds tousled, tufted, torn

Always when a boy I knew
the glory that the clouds upthrew
the curl in the cumulo
the puff in the cirro few

## Quits

the night he decided to call it quits

he arranged his affairs, packed his clothes

he never wanted to cause any trouble, any pain

in the sunshine he was always standing in the rain

## The Lord's Hand

The hand of the Lord is a gentle hand
the prick of the mighty thorn
blood droplets globed in gentleness and peace
for the thorn's wound is true

The Lord will not deny you
will not, like you, defy you,
though in your folly He descry you

the children that He loves
in spite of the evil that He loathes

the beauty of the rose is crowned with thorns
the prick of the thorn is a gentle warning
unlike the scratch of barb or bramble
from the truth in desperation we run
over fences or through undergrowth we scramble
from the one to the one we have not won

halting to destroy and wrench asunder
the bones and sinews He has knit
declining to blast with fire and thunder
the words of truth and grace that He has writ

## The Spoils

when the spoils had been divided
the benefactor denied
they drove away in trucks,
then stopped at their own places
and pulled their handbrakes on

## The Man

The man who wanted to create

built his house upon the sand.

Great was the fall

of the house upon that land.

# Voyage

Docilely the woman went with me
across the land of ice and heather.
Her heels were high in the puddles that she stepped
in the surly, non-committed weather.

But the room we left was lighted well,
there were plumes in coffee-cups and cigarettes.
Conviviality and intercourse
and many an invited guest.

I laid my hand upon her arm
in rooms so warm and gaily peopled.
Her skin was cold and goose-pimpled,
knowing the land iced and church-steepled.

Stopping by a ridge in cold country
I saw how her feet were tending
towards the open country offering
that the way was without ending.

Why she should wish to go with me
and why I should wish to go with her,
none could say. Who led us here?
And was it me or was it her?

Self-manifested at my side
in the short black coat she wore
and the heels either high or low
and the pained and damaged smile she wore

and her eyes almost ring-circled
and her wishing to smile and love
but her heart was sinking as it rose
and there were other voices rising above

She knew the way and had the key,
the key to the place where keys could not be used,
and the way was like the rest,
our paths were equal. We were abused.

## Becalmed

Here on the seas of the big city
the boats are becalmed.
Storms threaten in the western sky
but the air about us remains windless
the stillness is the punishment
the distant rumbling like a car not starting
the affirmation of the punishment
the powers that be working on far away.
Distant commotion confirms the stillness of our trouble

## Sleep

I woke and wished to sleep again.
to burrow under dreams,
greedy for forgetfulness,
dreams covering me like leaves.

But sleep ran from me like a river,
that steadfast, but obsolete lover,
the despair in my heart I would not quench,
that infinite agony we cannot fence
here with earth's temporal luxuries
buried deep in the warmth of pillows.

## Old Furniture

In the old alley I saw
squadrons of old furniture
wood and cloth the insects gnaw
surrendered to nature

The grass grew long and lean
the legs it wove about.
Human bodies never were seen
to lounge and lay them out.

It seemed they were for sale,
these contraptions ranged around.
From one house to the next to pale
in someone else's lounge-room.

The ghosts of those who lounged before
in the alley palely loitered:
who now were richer once were poor,
the poorer now exploited;

surprised by such activity
of grass that grew and weeds that wove
on the alley's slight acclivity
of chairs below and stoves above

One block further on there were
people eating breakfast
in the sun without a stir
of wind, consuming very steadfast.

Old furniture put up for sale
and left out in the rain
Old furniture come high weather or hail,
fills and spills the old lane.

Whether poor or poorer
you will find your seating eaten
by termite or wood-borer
and your every project beaten

## The Apple-trees

in the garden they planted apple-trees
— intention innocent, but the fruit forbidden
guileless the song that blew on the breeze
unsuspected the sorrow lain hidden

within the budding, the worm-bitten fruit
green globe forming within the ashen leaf
unseen the worm drove coiling at the root
gnawing at glory, sowing the seeds of grief

for many years God's favour was with them
favour many years ago given and bestowed
blessing each plant, each herb, each root and stem
but too heavy the spell, too heavy the load

of the easily accessible apple-tree
not just once and forever the deceit,
the design, the device curled about the tree
not banished forever the prospect of defeat

the advent of the worm, its rudeness,
flesh abandoned and accursed
diving into the dark for death or lewdness,
in the endlessness of night atrocious

the smoky jacket, the shiny skin
in the logic of the heart and mind
concealed what was contained within
and who ever knew a man born blind?

## An Experience

I had a strange experience and heard myself spoken about
while my back was turned, in the café of the room,
strange story of one who had stayed out
too long in the rain, in the hail, in the old grey gloom.

Now it was sunny weather, now the news had dried
on the curled yellow paper where the words were written
how I had most certainly either lived or died
what did it matter to the hardly bitten

Thus the tale had wafted back to them without a clue
from the doomscape landscape far and wide
of very nearly all I had gone through.
Some part of the story sad had been descried

But so little cared they that I was the one
who sat right by them, with my back to them turned,
that they turned to me as if for fun,
no self-connection whatsoever at all discerned

They were strange days that we had sojourned
in spite of so many beings sprung upon a planet
none in the slightest mite seemed at all concerned
to save a soul of the slightest merit

And I sat there strange to all connection
even to my own that was in the story told
egregiously to escape all detection
to be even lost within the fold

# Border Town

People are used to living in Border Town
The lights are up but the shutters are down
in Border Town

The slow wheels turn,
the night lights burn
in Border Town

The bush borders round
the continual sound
of people ignoring
the incessant warring
of Border Town

You dream in the caravan's corner
the years of the leaves of trees
brushing over you
—the memory of the dead,
the message of the living
flickering past you

When the sun comes up and the feet walk down
when the day begins and the night has ended
then you drive away from Border Town

Not a word was whispered, not a soul befriended.

You have not come here to live, you have not come here to die
but to pass on, on the sighing road winding on,
the unseen ending of the road, the shimmer of the rise
from the rising to the setting of the sun

This is how you came and went
from Border Town.

# The Birds

Early in the evening the bird broke
against the windscreen. The beauty of the car's speed
broke the beauty of the bird's throat
— glory of the feathers of the bird's need.

The birds clustered on the road
— congregations on the man-made thoroughfare.
Patterns of colour grouped together showed
kingfisher, house pigeon, crow, pink and grey galah

The as yet unfettered creatures of the air
— not the broken ferocity of the tiger or the bear,
their kingship disappointed of a lair,
their mastery truly without a forest to pace in

when man is master of the wood and stream
and the tall timbers' forest's back is broken

But the birds flock down undetected,
for the warmth of the road,
in swirls of colour without a sound,
while the majesty of the night rolls on

and the car continues on

## The Great World

Beyond one's door the great world beckons
— a place to get lost in, to be 'renewed'.
When adventure calls, or poverty threatens
— in the great world fresh chances may be pursued

— not realizing beyond one's door the air is thick
with indecision, a deepening swamp there's no
wading within; that love grows sick
in streets unable to detect their own woe.

In the East are the famous caravans,
sultans and sheikhs, fables of the desert sands;
the brisk bright breeze of ornamental fans,
mysteriously assembled by those alien hands.

And the rumour of the deep, great ocean,
bruised dark, glimmered blue, wreathed in foam,
the moving waters' continual commotion
where the vehicles of ships may roam.

The valleys of the sea are still unknown
beyond the reach of human insolence.
Only the ghosts of old sailors graze and groan,
surfing the waves in the sun's indolence.

And still the rumour of the land is calling
— the possible interest in human clustering.
Great cities are besieged, kingdoms falling,
the horizon of the world is burning, the wind is westering.

Then the fame and wonder of the West
— the spirits and treasures of the woods;
where what has been thought and said and done is best
— packaged produce of the mind and soul's goods.

So the great world with us still, beckons thus,
a fact undeniable, an ascertainable truth;
the great world revolves, requisitioning us,
called forth to action, to demonstrate our worth;

a source of legend, a never-ending tale
— a means merely to strike out,
the wild shirt whips billows in a gale,
journeying without light, drowned, beyond doubt.

But the great world now refuses to allow
one foot outside the door, step beyond the hold.
The air is thick, the streets are inundated now,
with no way new from the days of old.

No place is now to roam beyond the place at which you sit,
in the freedom of your room if you're in luck.

Dust floats undetected, no monitor counts the grit:
collocations of junk stir the muck.

Strike out, then, traveller, be true.
Death at your door, the poison streets are death.
Lies will cripple, corruptions will undo;
fact will vanish, lungs will fail your breath.

This is all, this is all you now will have.
The great world laughs, the great world has revenge
from east to west, from before to beyond the grave;
waves welter, sun's heat magnifies, and times change.

## Sweet Night

It was a sweet night.

The sky was low,

the stars like diamonds round my neck.

# The Pretty Schoolteacher

Farewell to the pretty schoolteacher
in the patent leather shoes,
so charming and so caring
to the little schoolchildren.

She changed her name
from Archer to Davis
and then she left us.
She was different in those last few days,
as if the time were permanently changing.
Did she spy with her eye
the disappointment of the class?

The mood was congratulatory
— the community consented,
warmth and cool in the suburbs
to the pretty schoolteacher
who changed her name,
her hair and her habit,
before she left us.

From the mistress beneath the flagpole on the dais
to the headmaster with the strap,
who agreed with the decision
of the pretty schoolteacher.
And so farewell!

## Those Days

Do you remember the days
when we were excited by our skill
— entrenched in a thousand ways,
fearless, running over the hill?

## The Music

Either the amoeba gathered the notes
or the notes comprehended the cells.
The song restored order on the life and motes
or the player was the life tinkling random bells.

# People

One amongst the others you see
who to and fro comes and goes
brooding like a cloud at sea
— clouts of sound he never knows.
His countenance is controlled
but desire debunks his reason.
Often his gaze cannot withhold
a tortured look quite out of season.

The others there are unaware
but to me it's all too clear
— he's bored and pale, without being there,
his words he cannot steer.
Platforms where no one assembles,
night passes without event,
and then one's fellow man resembles
spirits and shades, subterranean sent.

## Homework

For learning I was sent to school
to get by heart each precious rule.
Only by marks could the race be won.
I wished to win, so I did run.

Long hours I sat inside a room,
lost in pages, a gathering gloom.
No one told me what it was for,
but we were sorry, we were poor.

## She

Then I saw her face suffused with anger

— no way of knowing who put the pang there.

Her brows contracted,

her eyes distracted,

her feet finding their way past me.

But once her face came forth with sorrow

— a look that she could not lend or borrow

— her lips turned down,

her brow in frown,

her heart finding its way toward me.

## A Letter

I dropped a letter on the stair

and my shoe immediately stepped there

on the inscription of a hand

from a once-lived-in land.

Though of augury I was not sure,

yet I felt the allure

of some omen signalled there

— the onset of an unknown despair.

## The Season's Song

We should have followed them
for the sake of the song they sang
— happy in the hearts of
the wending away young.

We heard them in the first place
from the stairs of the first floor landing.
And they sang with a carefree grace
a song without an ending.

In the streets of the foreign city
like a charm in a wood,
the spell of a modern ditty,
the song went on for good.

And then we heard them on
the heaving of a ferry crossing
when night was closing in,
and black waves were tossing.

Yet their voices rose above
the ancient stone and brickwork
— some joy that pursued us,
among the honoured stone and fretwork.

Pursued us as a cloud.

The song was not sad,
no pang of tears,
deep-down our hearts were glad

— for the tune of the time,
for the notes together strung
— happy in the hearts of
the wending-away young.

# One

She would always be by his side.
How lightly she walked as though on air
in soft white shoes and jeans.
Why was her walk so light
when her husband stolidly trod so near?
Made from a rib, or made from air?
He thought his world too small for care.
He was angry, to be boxed in such a square,
but this was not what it was all about.
She knew, without the nagging of a doubt,
they had it all, no need to hanker,
no need to pine, in an envious rancour.
A home, a child, a community, a life;
a husband: and she would always be his wife;
no enemy, no stranger at the door;
no one in uniform, to enforce the law.
her walk was light, as light as air
— made from a rib or made from air.
She would always be by his side
— to work in unison, to gently glide.
The bench needs cleaning, it is done
— this was a life just made for one.

## Tattoo

Inner-city maudlin depressed at fifteen
she left school for the wide emptiness of all
ending the schoolyard melodrama queen
for fresh fields forever, all creatures great or small.

She got a tattoo on her upper arm
covering the whole white surface quite
— a fantastic design of frenzied alarm;
dark veins of stillness fixed, blood's flood in spite.

Many years now, it was, since she'd paid the price
for the artist's savage realism he drew
the sure significance of the knife's advice
carving the selected pattern to imbue.

Still for her the fashion had not faded
She wore it still, it did, she could recall
choosing the design in sizes graded
in the shop's glare, on the old display wall

It was the kind of thing her friends were with
to illustrate a sign's calligraphy;
to wind in time, while into time you live;
writing once for all in old orthography

She drank with friends when it happened to her
— a spontaneous desire to impress
— a tinctured picture, as the booze ran through her
— thus to be ensigned like all the rest

The tattoo was a bold idea at first
— to impress the pretty pattern on her skin
without taking thought for this day or the next,
merely entering the fiery emblem deep within.

She did not look for how it then would be
— in later years, when the fashion faded
— to unpick the complex tapestry
that the artist's brazen knife had bladed.

For the present she wanted nothing more
than to wear the fiery emblem all abroad,
displaying it boldly so that everyone saw
the dragon slain by the hero with a sword

She did not see how the mind would concentrate
on the meaning of the etched extravagance
fearing an inevitable approaching fate:
seeking to revise its sharp significance

And now it was so long since friends had quitted
the society and scenes she'd sought and savoured;

yet the emblem was so deeply pained and pitted
the device so deeply scored and graven

In those days none had ever disapproved
the style of the legend she had chosen.
Everyone had unanimously enthused
about the decoration when she showed them.

So she'd melted into their midst unperturbed,
even as the tattoo's lines of ink done merged
into feints and flourished undisturbed
by any need for dear salience urged

She had a boyfriend then unemployed
like she was. They stayed home and saw no need
for aims and ambitions to be deployed
— that was all just futility and greed.

There was no future beyond living on the dole
— those free handouts were more than enough
to line the pockets, satisfy the soul,
considering all the piles of other stuff

— more barbecues at council offices
and sausage sizzles on the local green,
than alternative lurks, government promises
in any city street or suburban scene;

or vice versa—didn't matter which.
Important thing was being on the hook
— to cure every ailment, scratch or itch,
before the doctor even had to look.

You loaded up hourly like a Christmas tree
with every wish you could ever want
— and all good things were to be had for free
— why strain and sweat in the poverty stunt.

But then, surprised, one day the call came through:
she would have to go to work, earn her pay;
leaving the lover lingering in the stew.
She could not be idle and any longer stay.

An office job, in a city building;
hours nine to five six days every week;
necessitating new friends and clothing,
replacing the dole queue with boutique.

Large distance from her boyfriend then it proved
to be, who stayed unemployed, a down and out.
She drifted from the one she thought she loved,
finding others with whom to hang about.

So she lost touch with all her group of friends,
adopting new ways she had not thought before;

and she started then to foresee new ends,
new trends, new means she would not ignore.

she got used to working in town each day,
catching the train early in the morning,
when the sun broke out in common clay,
and the first heat in the clouds was burning.

The routine set in and seemed set for good,
conforming to the pressures round about;
confirming herself on this different road.
She took to leaving the one she could do without.

She met her boyfriend only time to time,
drinking in the pub on the corner bend.
For what had happened he was not to blame
—all imperfections must come to an end.

He seemed somewhat sorry to see her go;
his own situation was still out of luck.
They both felt they had been quite close,
but it seemed impossible now to have her back.

"Things seem so much different now," she told him,
"with a job and everything changed to this.
How now can what we had ever be the same;
how can we return to what now we miss

— of friends I am no longer with or spend
less time with now or never see at all.
I don't see that we can begin to mend
the fences or break down this wall."

So they parted and went their separate ways,
seeing of each other still less and less,
till she saw no return to former days,
reversion to that hardship from her new success.

Her new friends at first said nothing much
about the tattoo when they saw it now and then.
They'd reach out a hand perhaps to touch
the lines of the pattern on her skin

and ask her when she'd had it done and why.
Of that she could not really conceive or think
though in lengthy explanations she'd try
to find the reason for the marks of ink.

She did not mind what their sight might see;
no regard seemed critical in its bent.
What they might find there they could take for free;
she never dreamed that any hurt was meant.

So time still passed, and she grew older
— more conservative, more conforming to it all.

She did not remember if she'd once been bolder,
or if the changes made were large or small.

She merely blended with the company she kept,
compelled by what by what to do, to be like them;
no time to think from when she worked or slept;
too busy meeting schedules, making friends.

She hardly looked at how she began to seem;
whether her look struck people differently
from how she formerly had for so long been,
from what they once saw but now could see;

and when she looked, gave mind, received a shock
at the sight of the new self that there emerged;
yet the old person walked behind the image struck,
still as a ghost that the whole frame disturbed.

Then illness happened, and she stayed at home
— a minor problem, it seemed to be at first.
She only needed to spend some time alone
some days to mend, she thought, but all got worse.

The disease took hold of her whole system.
She succumbed to the pressure of its weight.
The doctors did not know in their wisdom
how to arrest her present state.

So down she swirled into sickness' pool
like many levels crumbling of an endless dream
— history collapsing as the lost travellers fell,
body tumbling where never-fading torches gleam.

At the week's end, she rang to say
she still was not well, time was needed yet
before she mended and could meet the day,
before the fever ended and her temper set;

but still another week and still the same
— the illness' rampancy she had not gleaned;
the gouts of frailty that rent her frame,
like the unimagined onslaught of a fiend;

and then another week and still in this way on,
till weeks were months and months became a year.
The doctors came, looked at her, and were gone,
opining that her life's end was near.

Thus it is that sometimes events occur
that change the courses of the lives we've led
and the pattern we imagined is disturbed
and something else transpires instead.

At first friends came to see how she would be,
expecting that she soon would mend and then

she'd return to her former busy ways and means,
and the old routine would just apply again.

But she did not mend, and so still they came,
and came often, while the disease was new;
yet later this first frequency did wane,
when infirmity increased and grew.

She could see how they slowly slipped away,
how the brightness of their arrival soon would dim,
when the company they kept was gone to grey,
and life now dour and dull, as it should seem.

She was left alone, with none who cared,
except the doctors on their scheduled rounds,
who looked at her, diagnosed, and despaired
she'd ever overcome her body's wounds.

They developed a special healing plan,
designed to restore her to her former health;
authorities employed a helping hand
to bring her into bed or run her bath.

Paid persons would be the last to forget
the patient listed on the routine books;
in the work there is a licence to neglect
someone for whom you toil and clean and cook.

These continued coming, at appointed hours,
while friends, acquaintances drifted on,
showing how soft sweet society sours
when sudden sickness sings her siren song.

Four years went by and still no sign appeared
her constant level ailment would relieve
— either to lift entirely or to clear
or make a steady progress to the grave.

But she died, and yet the tattoo remained,
an image driven deep into her soul.
The body lying there was but stained
— showing or not showing its final toll.

## Thermometers

Thermometers once told bodies of their flame
— how the fever burned, how the temper soared.
It was lucid when cool to warmer came
— in the slender glass where the stuff was stored.

This was before the wholesale meltdown of the mind,
collapsing the struts and structures that upheld,
releasing slats of construct like the rain and wind;
before all direction was siphoned off the world.

Bodies then were kept within our tender care,
carefully regulating the least upset,
when out of place was the least degree or hair
or cold was seizing and broke out in sweat.

But now all's fed into the fire, all's hot;
seasons squeeze into a final summer;
fevers rise and rage until forgot
and flames are fuelled in any manner.

**THIS IS JUST A NOTE
TO SAY THAT YOU
NEEDN'T READ THIS
POEM AS IT IS
— SO SHORT & SO SWEET
ONLY ONE WORD**

long
(BUT READ THE TITLE
(OPTIONAL))
(SO SWEET & SO SHORT)

## Night Sky

at the day's end blueness emptied from the sky
and the grey clouds scudded, coasting like sailboats,
on the darkness before the stars.

The clouds marched across the sky,
their billowing shapes obscuring the twinkling of the stars,
moored in the blue withering to a bruise,
anchored in the firmament of fate,
piloting fixed station light.

and I looked away
and the clouds' consciousness was filled
when I turned back again,
from my thoughts which merrily danced amongst the stars.
The clouds still scraped their bellies across the canopy of trees,
swirled with commotion conjured from afar,
their sails still full,
their rags still pressed against the night.

# A Summer's Sunday

He must have been a jolly fellow in his time
— the old chap in suit of chocolate-brown
and thin silvery hair-pieces.
He can still whip up a jig
to the summer's brass band,
still heave a salute
to the sergeant of shadows,
still discover a dance for life-time's old sake.

So what is wrong with you
that you are sitting and fearing
his down-at-heel graces
and wild, tottering advances
(though we are smiling to see
his clownish fellow-well-met
to a child who has wandered more closely to see
this funny fool-phantom
of summer's descanting)
for, once, were we not, as jolly as he?

## Heaven's Waiting-room

Their bodies have departed
years ago. All that is left now

are frail souls the wind would lift
and take from us

but that something keeps them here,
fluttering, breasting the wind,

hand in another,
delicately as butterflies

and the voices of children.

# Hurricane

The hurricane contorts

to a pirouette

and flexes all to its shape

— just like a washing machine,

only different.

# Exam

In the room gathered

the variegated wanderings of the crowd.

Nervousness reigned

to keep us silent,

and on each face

and in each bosom

the incipient terror of the unknown

— on each face the question begging,

"Where are we going?

What lies ahead?"

## Museum

By the Hermes statue

in the potential darkness of the room

the carved milk-white faces

of the Roman people

— a hand in the bridle of a horse,

the curling locks of man and woman.

Even under the fist of oppression

the hand delighting to hold

the bone hair-comb,

the metal serving-ring.

## Lines: By Philip Larkin's House

At the end of a journey
— this quiet house, as part of a row.
Nothing more

than a usual house, in a usual place
— with trees, flowers, walls;
a garden glove trodden to a claw.

Then we are left with present absences
(the sun falling through a spate of trees,
making a heart in garden):

*Things seem to happen and are appropriate*
*— our lives become us, will or no.*
*There are no accidents, and nothing's sudden.*

# The Cardplayers

(Luxembourg Gardens, Paris)

Seagulls wheel above the beachless city.
Trees crane stiffly, bare of leaves,
in the scarlet light of the garden's grandeur.

We come to sit and watch and stroll;
gossip in this ancient city,
where time is set in stone.

And here, too, the cardplayers come,
bundled in coats and scarves,
the sun's laughter in their bones.

But they have seen the joke
— how the standing stones
can tumble.

From the botched and knuckled hands
the cards are falling
as patiently as leaves.

## The Garden

The sun marks you out,
seems to upbraid you
for having wandered from this place—

garden of unclipped grass,
tranquil as a frenzy
in a photograph.

Tomato vines send out
a hand of clutching fingers
round no throat.

Two white chairs
and a table
are knee-deep in grasses.

You are irresolute, sick
with indecision;
you seem to be

between two seasons,
and the sun's closed fist,
vibrant with unresting anger,

unfolds no simple answer.
Behind you the house
in waiting accepts

the message of the giant city.
*It is nearly spring.*
*Winter is almost passed.*

*Turn back inside:*
*Renew your purpose,*
*the years are turning over.*

## Graduation Day

They appear as bats
perched the right side up

and blinking in daylight;
their actions are muffled in folds.

Their caps are eggcups inverted
and their smiles chips in the egg.

Tassels, thin as horsetails,
whip their cheeks at each turning.

A constant need for adjustment:
their mortarboards lift in the wind.

Their diplomas are telescopes
not held to the eye.

Parents banter and jostle,
the thin whine of cameras.

The whites of their smiles
pass through lenses

and into uncertainty:

the dense black spaces of man.

# Between Four Walls

I think dreams must take the shape
of houses; our desires must assume
the aspect of rooms — a separate space

for each thing to be done,
so sleep cannot appear as hunger,
nor speculation be confused with television.

And only doors provide the unity
of access — hinges to admit,
hinges to omit.

Can it be maintained, such fidelity,
such unwavering patience
of bare walls and floorboards,

  austerely composed to receive
  like a good listener
  rebuffing passion?

## Puddle

Chug of buses, cars' expectoration,
footpath dissected with directions,
chocolate wrappers round her feet.

This is reflection in her eyes

— her tears turning the blue
of her nurse's dress
a deeper spotted blue.

## Now

Now there is again the opening
and closing of doors

— hard objects thrown against
the incomplete, the wind rushes through.

We have given so much of ourselves
to each other, the only regret

is the tears you shall cry for me
which I will not see or feel.

Dials, clocks and watches!
My dastardly silence!

## Waves

Walking from the caravan park
I came upon the beach near dark,
like something I'd discovered.

Rocks climbed into the swell.
The sand, like a scarf flung out,
winged away in the distance.

The clouds' grey brow furrowed low
on the horizon, to allow
one inverted V of light,

like an oasis far out.

Mourning dress: the hem of the sea
lost momentum on the sand, slipped back.
The waves were weary on the shore,

and seemed to cry far out.

# Picture Frame

No storm blew, that night
you showed a picture frame
— your lidded look of pride;
my frozen portable face.

The clouds banked low
and I rained upon your head
— like melting wax/ I glowed
for the body shed.

But the lid of cloud only freed
the collared sky — that day
I turned around and found
you'd taken the picture out.

# Letter

So I lick the sweetened gum,

and the letter is complete.

Each sentence runs smooth,

the words reined and bridled in,

nuances checked with soft lift

of hand and tongue-click.

False starts and scorings-out

I have omitted—stuttering

is not a social grace.

A conversation across seas,

my lips left open for weeks.

Impotence will grip you

— you'll vandalize the seal,

grab the letter by the throat.

But put the letter in your desk.

All we'll hear is hooves

knocking stable-doors at night

as we warm our feet by the fire.

## King's Cross

Drunks roll slow to the passing feet.
Like new-hatched chicks, flap
groggy wings, feel the new heart's beat.

Theirs is an ancient law
— jackets grained with dirt
brought by shoes from a distant shore.

And the historical account
their beards' calligraphy
has carefully written out.

# The Truth

Once we were lovers
And my love for you was true.
  Why, then, were you false?
When love is truth, truth is love:
  Both these things not two but one.

## Memento

You cut a tress
out of your hair,
to wound and bless
as we stood there

— to keep the lock
in safest place:
a tender shock
if I should face

the love that's lost
the love that's gone
now double-crossed
and cheated on.

So near the end
of you and me:
our God won't send
the second tree.

The well-met chance
that passed us by;
our first romance
will only die:

for we'll not find
again one time
scope to rewind
the first-place crime;

for you and me
we're locked into
inseparably
to see it through

unless you have
cause to believe
what once was love
is why we grieve.

The salty crust
of vanished years
is all the dust
of endless tears.

## Autumn's Leaves

I would gather up all the leaves of autumn,
all the little leaves red, yellow and brown.
Yes, I would gather all of autumn's leaves
in order to feel complete.
I would spy into the joys of summer
those mere swelterings in the heat
when memory was alive and life was sweet.
And I would foresee all of winter's woes
when branches are bare
and the heart wrung dry.
I would gather all the leaves of autumn,
calculating the soul's account,
before casting them to the constant wind.

Made in the USA
Monee, IL
10 July 2023

d8eb4196-7e7b-4c7a-9baf-f13bdf0c7157R01